TAKE ME
TO MISSOURI

TAKE ME
TO MISSOURI

Charles E. Fair

To order additional copies of this book, contact:
Xlibris Corporation
1-888-795-4274
www.Xlibris.com
Orders@Xlibris.com
99734

CONTENTS

DEDICATION

This book is dedicated to love, and all of the people that provided me care and others like me, who could not have survived without their loving care. I am especially grateful to my wife, Ramona Fair and my five children. I include others on my dedication list like my father, Calvin Fair, my four siblings, doctors, nurses, nurse's aids, ministers of the gospel, Christian brothers and sisters, kind strangers, devoted staff of Children's Home Society, and members of Toastmasters.

ACKNOWLEDGEMENTS

I would like to thank God for giving me hope in the midst of a seemingly hopeless situation, and bringing kind, loving people into my life, to help me see, as well as to experience the wonders of love and the universal reality that not only do I need God, but I need to be mindful that my dependence on other people is an essential facet of life.

It is with great joy that I pause to recognize some important people that in one way or another enriched my life and contributed to the completion of this book. First, many thanks is given to my father Calvin E. Fair and my mother the late Mrs. Lillie Mae Fair, my sister Francis A. Fair and brothers Reverend James C. Fair, Eddie L. Fair and Michael E. Fair.

Great love and appreciation is extended to my dear wife Ramona, who endured great hardship and rendered invaluable service to me, when I could not help myself. Also I would like to thank my children Charmaine N. Fair, Jasmine L. Fair, Jerome C. Fair, and Jamal T. Fair for the care they rendered me and continue to assist me in my time of need. I am also grateful to the love shown me by my son Charles E. Fair, Jr.

Special thanks is offered to Valerie Bahim, David Langley, Willie Clowers, Jeanie Hardwick, James Hill, Donald Lyons, Earl Kitchchings, Truman Sigler, Gene Hollowmon, Khamil Ojoyo and all those members of Toastmasters that were instrumental in my growth and development as a speaker and loving and caring person.

Dr. Cora Adams, Dr. Ann Berliner, Dr. S. Kapoor, Dr. Gordon Cappelletty, Dr. Robert Foster, Pastor Sylvester Small, Dr. Lily Small, Mr. Michael Cox, Mr. Alcedro Rabsatt, Dr. Robert Mikel and the late Dr. Keith Standing influence in my life is deeply appreciated.

Sister Eleanor Hammond, Brother Givens, Brother Melvin Hayes, Brother Terry McNeill and Minister Warren Hodge are all dedicated children for the cause of love.

Dr. Barome of Shands deserves the award for compassion, courage and excellence for his devotion to humanity and especially to me and my family.

Abraham, Othelia, Cedro, Larry and family your love is greatly appreciated. Ella Parham from Arkansas, your kindness was not forgotten.

Joseph Jackson, Linda Rudd, Karen Hamilton, Rick Ortiz, Stella Botello, John Mauro and Janet Bouffard are dedicated to the care of the least of these in our society.

Aunt Jurdine, Funteller, Rev. Lorenzo, Uncle Roosevelt, Uncle Lonnie, Aunt Mable, Derrick, Michael, Aunt Janie, Uncle Walter Fair, his son Thomas A. Fair, Irma, Anette, Vanessa, Gail, Shirley Ann, Mark Hunter, Aunt Bessie, Sandra, Bonita, Mary L. Hope, Annie Poe, Jacqueline Vaughn, Debra McCarter, Larry D. Fair, Sonja Fair, Katherine Lowery, Wayne Dexter Fair, Priscilla Randle, Ethel Williams, Bernard, Mattie, Bernard, Jr., Leonard, the late Gregory Williams and Sister Gwendolyn, Benny Bell, Robert Parker, David Lamar Fair and to all of the members of my family and friends that were omitted, your contributions are not forgotten.

Finally to two of my newest friends Brother Emanuel and Sister Shirley Haynes contributions to the completion of this book is immense. Brother Haynes words of encouragement helped me to better cope with some very difficult life challenges. I thank God for him. His implicit trust in me as a person is refreshing. His vision of reaching the masses for Jesus is inspiring. His love and appreciation of his wife's skills have in a major way touched my life.

Sister Shirley Haynes has spent hours of her time working with me to correct my mistakes and turn this book into God's best. Sister Shirley, thank you for the work you put into making this book one that will be read and appreciated by millions of people all over the world.

Take Me To Missouri

On August 28, 1963 a famous Baptist preacher stood before the Lincoln Memorial and shared with the nation a dream he had. Today I stand before you and declare that I also have a dream. That one day men and women, boys and girls will take a trip to Missouri.

Now, I imagine that many of you are asking this question. Charles, out of all of the beautiful places in which one can visit, why Missouri? Why not visit Hawaii, Paris, Fresno, Jacksonville or even Middleburg, Florida.

Now for those of you who are not familiar with Missouri, it is known as the "show me state", but "Missouri" as it is referred to in this message refers to love.

Why Missouri? The Apostle Paul's reply to this question was short but clear. He implies, 'without love I am nothing'. We see this all over America and all over the world. People seek to find their purpose in life outside of God. We see this in people's quest to accumulate wealth, only to discover that no amount of money can replace that place reserved for God. We see this in mankind's search for pleasure. Some seek to find the meaning in life via drugs, only to discover that the more drugs you use the more you want and that no lasting experience can be found in drug abuse. Some seek to find fulfillment in immoral sexual encounters, only to discover that as good as sex may feel, apart from God, this lasts only for a season and it brings with it infinite deadly consequences. Love is the source of life that makes life worthwhile.

Take Me To Missouri deals with two types of love. First, we have natural expressions of love; like kindness, patience, and unselfishness. Then we have God's expression of love which is seen when Jesus gave his life for the sins of humanity.

Now that we know why we need love, let us turn our attention to our second point. "What is Missouri"? In the third chapter of the gospel of John, we find these prophetic words:

"For God so loved the world that he gave
His only begotten son, that whosoever
Believeth in him should not perish but have everlasting life."

Isaiah the prophet's response to this question is

"Surely he hath bourne our grief and carried our sorrows . . .
he was wounded for our transgressions. He was bruised for our
iniquities and the chastisement for our peace was upon him and
by his stripes we are healed."

Christ says in John 13:34-35:

"A new commandment I give unto you,
That ye love one another; as I have loved you, that ye also love
one another.

By this shall all men know that ye are my disciples if ye have love
one to another."

My daughter, Jasmine knows about Missouri. When Jasmine was in elementary school, she was a member of her school band.

One day she came home from school all excited. She quickly came to me and said, "Daddy, take me to Missouri."

Now those aren't the exact words that Jasmine shared, but what Jasmine really said was this. "Daddy our school band is going to be playing at a school that is not far from where we live. I would like for you to be there."

When her request was made, I was working full time with socially, economically and educationally disadvantaged children. Now after work I looked forward to going home, relaxing, watching television, or reading the paper. Going to some event after working eight hours was not my way of relaxing. However guess what happened on the day of Jasmine's event? I took Jasmine to Missouri. By attending her event and showing Jasmine that her dad really cares for her.

Not to be out done, during my final semester of gradate school, I found myself in need of some money to pay my tuition. School may well be a place for education, but I am here to tell you that if you don't pay your tuition, you are not allowed to enroll in the classes being offered.

I paused and thought who do you know that loves you enough to help you? Who is able to help you? My dad came to mind. I called my dad and I said, "Daddy, take me to Missouri." Now that is not what I said to my father. Actually I said, "Dad I need several hundred dollars to pay my final semester tuition. Will you loan me the money?"

My dad said, "Son, I was going to give you a gift for graduation. I will send you the money for your tuition." He continued, "You don't have to pay me back." It will be your graduation present." I thanked my dad. Every now and then he was reminded of his kindness to his son.

Now that we know why we need love, and we know what love is, let us turn our attention to our third and final point. When

Missouri? The answer to this question is found in II Corinthians 6:2b:

> *"Behold, now is the accepted time; behold, now is the day of salvation."*

The truth of this passage was brought home to me as a young soldier. Prior to going to basic training, I visited my uncle Lee Andrew. I told my uncle I would see him after my training was complete, but I was never going to see my uncle alive again. While in basic training, the news was brought to me that my uncle was killed in a tragic motorcycle accident. This sudden loss of my uncle caused me great anguish and grief. The uncertainty of life and its brevity was clear.

One Tuesday Brother Campbell greeted me at the door of the church, as he had done many times before. I looked forward to seeing him on Friday. He was not at Church on Friday. On Sunday my wife shared with me that brother Campbell passed away on Friday. Once again, the preciousness and uncertainty of a person's physical life was made clear.

Finally, in life we will have opportunities to tell people how much we care about them. But if we don't take time to show love and take people to "Missouri", a lot of people will be wondering if we really care. Don't just talk about love, show your love. This is what it means to "take me to Missouri."

In I John 4:7-10 you will find what God means by 'Missouri'.

> *"Beloved, let us love one another: for love is of God; and every one that loveth is born of God, and knoweth God.*
> *He that loveth not knoweth not God; for God is love.*
> *In this was manifested the love of God toward us, because that God sent his only begotten Son into the world, that we might live through him.*
> *Herein is love, not that we love God, but that he loved us,*
> *And sent his Son to be the propitiation for our sins."*

A Good Touch

L et's turn to the scripture in Mark 5:25-34 and read.

> *"And a certain woman, which had an issue of blood twelve years,*
> *and had suffered many things of many physicians, and had spent*
> *all that she had, and was nothing better, but rather grew worse.*
> *When she had heard of Jesus, came in the press behind, and touched*
> *his garment. For she said, 'If I may touch but his clothes,*
> *I shall be whole.' And straightway the*
> *Fountain of her blood was dried up; and she felt in her body that*
> *she was healed of that plague. And Jesus, immediately knowing*
> *in himself that virtue had gone out of him, turned him about in*
> *the press, and said, 'Who touched my clothes?'*
> *And his disciples said unto him, Thou seest*
> *The multitude thronging thee, and sayest thou, 'Who touched me?'*
> *And he looked around about to see her that had done this thing.*
> *But the woman fearing and trembling, knowing what was done in*
> *her, came and fell down before him, and told him all the truth.*
> *And He said unto her, 'Daughter, thy faith hath made thee whole;*
> *go in peace, and be whole of thy plague."*

There are times in life when one is confronted with a situation that requires a 'good touch'. The lady in the text is such a case.

She had what appeared to be an impossible physical condition. However, her faith in Jesus gave her the healing touch that she was in need of.

On August 13, 1984 I found myself in the hospital not as a patient, but as an observer. My wife, the patient was giving birth to our first born child. I was trying to console myself just in case she happened to give birth to a girl. Now, understand I have nothing against girls. I was in that mode to having a son. Girls are great. I now have two lovely daughters. Charmaine and Jasmine are very dear to my heart. However, for my first born I had hoped for, and longed for a son. The moment of truth came as the doctor announced, "It's a boy!" Joyfully I said, "Yes! Yes! Yes!" Ladies and gentlemen that was a "Good Touch."

Some of you may be wondering Brother Charles. What does your wife having a son have to do with a 'good touch'?

My wife, like some married women are expected to do what it is not in their power to do and that is to determine the sex of their children. All too often wives are unfairly blamed when men don't get the child they were expecting. If you happen to be one of those who was unfairly cited for something you had no control over, today if you reach out in faith you can experience a 'good touch' and offer forgiveness to such a person.

In the eighth chapter of the book of Mark, Mark 8:22-25, there is a very interesting story about a 'good touch'.

> *And he cometh to Bethsaida; and they bring a blind man unto him, and besought him to touch him.*
>
> *And he took the blind man by the hand, and led him out of the town; and when he had spit on his eyes, and put his hands upon him, he asked him if he saw ought.*
> *And he looked up, and said, I see men as trees, walking.*
> *After that he put his hands again and he was restored, and saw every man clearly.*

The story regarding the blind man receiving his sight reveals some possible insight that may help those who fail to see men as men. Could it be that the more time you spend with Jesus, the more you realize that Jesus is concerned about your individual care? He does desire for you to be whole.

Reflecting back as a little boy, I was born and raised in Jackson, Mississippi. I had very limited contact with white people. You see, when I was a little boy there was something known as segregation. White people lived in certain parts of town and blacks lived in another part of town. Therefore my limited interaction with whites led me to believe the stereotype that white people are bad.

Now something happened to me in the late 1960's. My family moved north. To my surprise we had a white neighbor. I was amazed that the white lady was nice. I had a hard time as a young boy trying to understand how a person could be white and nice. I thank God for allowing me to experience a life changing encounter. This also was a "Good Touch" from this kind woman and neighbor. You see, love is not limited to the color of a person's skin. Love can be, and is expressed by people of all skin colors who choose to be loving and caring.

Over thirty years ago my brother, Eddie was involved in a serious motorcycle accident. This accident took place less than three miles from our home. While I don't recall who took me to the scene of the accident. I do recall clearly seeing my brother motionless on the ground.

I ran to him, knelt down and pushed him on his shoulder and loudly called him by name, "Eddie, Eddie!" Then I heard the most momentous moaning that I have ever herd in my life. Eddie was crying out in pain, "ah, ah, ah!" Then I cried out, "He's a live. There is hope!"

The ambulance arrived. They allowed me to ride to the hospital in the ambulance. I was not prepared for what was to transpire during that ride to the hospital. I have heard my brother say many names as we were growing up. However, I don't ever recall him shouting out, "Jesus!" "Jesus!" In time of trouble Eddie called to Jesus. Jesus did not let him down. Jesus spared my brother's life. Again that was a "Good Touch."

I realize that life can be filled with "Good Touches" if we reflect and think about it. Another experience reaffirms this while I was a student at California State University-Fresno. One day after class I received word that my mother was seriously ill. It was not known how much longer she would be with us. I was preparing for a graduate examination at the time. It was the practice of many professors that if you don't take the examination on the day it was given, shame on you.

Anyway to my surprise when I explained my situation to my professor, he granted me permission to take the examination on a later date. This professor's compassion and understanding were great. My professor, Dr. Irv Ruhl's simple act of kindness showed me that he really cared about me as a person. As my social worker professor, he demonstrated the ability to transform his broad experiences in his field of study. This was a "Good Touch." for me. Because of this man's kindness to a child of God, nations will one day know the power of a 'good touch'.

I'd like for you to focus your attention on three life lessons we can learn from this passage. The first lesson we can learn from this lady is that she had an issue. Her issue happened to be a physical one. In life you are going to have problems. Today we see the massive loss of jobs. You will also realize that husbands and wives are having some issues. Parents have issues when their daughter brings home some strange looking man. She says to them, "He's just a friend." Employees have issues when their employer gives them their pay check a day or two late. The first lesson we should learn from this message is that these problems are a part of life.

The second lesson we should learn from this message is that some problems are beyond our natural ability to resolve. For instance, the lady referred to in our text had a physical problem that the doctor could not resolve. Today we have men and women who have put their lives on the line. Families all over America wonder if their love ones will return home safely from war. Only God is able to return soldiers home safely from battle.

The third lesson, and perhaps the most important lesson of the three, is to trust God. No matter how hopeless things may appear. Even during times in life when things from a natural view point seem hopeless, we must put our trust in God.

For example, the time I accepted Jesus Christ as my Lord and Savior. At this time I was attending a revival service. The preacher, Pastor F.O. Hockenhull preached the gospel. During the message I was convicted by what he shared. However, I thought, "If that preacher thinks that I am going to get up in front of the church and admit that I am a sinner, and give up having fun living in sin, and accept Jesus as my Savior, he's mistaken." "This is not going to happen."

I went home determined to continue in my selfish life style. Then something happened before that revival was over. How long was that revival? Was it three days, one week, or more? I don't recall. However, this I do know. Before that revival was over, I stood in front of the church in the midst of strangers and confessed that I am a sinner in need of God's forgiveness. I put my trust in God to save my soul from eternal doom. This was again, a "Good Touch."

Not only did God give me an abiding peace that when my body gives way, my soul has an eternal place to reside with God.

In addition, God opened my spiritual blinded mind. I saw how I was willing to risk temporary fun and pleasure to lose something priceless, my soul. Just as God intervened in my situation, you can also trust God to do the same for you. Just put your trust in Him. Accept Jesus as your personal Savior.

Put your trust in Him as Lord of your life. Then you too can have a "Good Touch."

Request Granted

As a young boy Solomon knew what it meant to have a request granted. He asked God for an understanding heart that he would be able to judge God's people with the ability to discern what is good and what is not. God was so pleased with Solomon's request that Solomon was given riches and honor in addition to understanding to discern judgment (I Kings 3:3-12).

"And Solomon loved the Lord, walking in the statutes of David his father . . . In Gibeon the Lord appeared to Solomon in a dream by night: and God said, Ask what I shall give thee.

And Solomon said, Thou hast shewed unto thy servant David my father great mercy, according as he walked before thee in truth, and in righteousness, and in uprightness of heart with thee; and thou has kept for him this great kindness, that thou hast given him a son to sit on this throne, as it is this day . . .

Give therefore thy servant an understanding heart to judge thy people (and) that I may discern between good and bad: for who is able to judge this thy so great a people?

And the speech pleased the Lord that Solomon had asked this thing. And God said unto him, Because thou has asked this thing, and hast not asked for thyself . . . but hast asked for thyself understanding to discern judgment;

Behold, I have done according to thy words: lo, I have given thee wise and an understanding heart . . . "

David also knew what it meant to have a request granted. One day he had to face a massive problem. He had to face a literal giant, who was known as Goliath. David put his trust in God to slay or resolve his problem. God rewarded David's trust in God (I Samuel 17:37-51).

> *"David said moreover, The Lord that delivered me out of the paw of the lion, and out of the paw of the bear, he will deliver me out of the hand of this Philistine.*
> *And Saul said unto David, Go, and the Lord be with thee . . .*
> *Then said David to the Philistine, Thou comest to me with a sword, and with a spear, and with a shield; but I come to thee in the name of the Lord of hosts, the God of the armies of Israel, . . .*
> *This day will the Lord deliver thee into mine hand; and I will smite thee, and take thine head from thee . . . that all the earth may know that there is a God in Israel . . .*
> *So David prevailed over the Philistine with a sling and with a stone, and smote the Philistine, and slew him; but there was no sword in the hand of David . . .*
> *And when the Philistines saw their champion was dead, they fled."*

David not only destroyed Goliath, he became one of the most beloved kings of Israel.

Today America is facing one of its most turbulent economic challenges of the 21st century. God is still true to His word. He will honor and provide for those who put their trust in Him. There was a man who was searching for a specific job. He put his faith in God to provide him that job. That man's faith was rewarded. He not only got a new job, he also got a pay raise as well.

Many, many years ago I was a shy little boy, who had a desire to become a public speaker. How on earth can a person become a good speaker if he is afraid to speak in public? Somehow, such a person must overcome their fear and develop the necessary confidence to stand in front of strangers and talk in public. God has transformed that once shy little boy into a blazing servant of God. When it comes to speaking about the goodness of God, I am honored that God has blessed me to speak to people outside of the church as well. God is true to His word. If you put your trust in God, God will never let you down.

> *"Delight thyself also in the Lord; and he shall give thee the desires of thine heart.*
> *Commit thy way unto the Lord; trust also in him; and he shall bring it to pass."* Psalms 37:4-5

When I was temporarily paralyzed, I longed to one day be able to walk again. That request has been granted. Finally, we have this example in I Chronicles:

> *"And Jabez called on the God of Israel, saying,*
> *Oh that thou wouldest bless me indeed, and enlarge my coast, and that thine hand might be with me, and that thou wouldest keep me from evil, that it may not grieve me!*
> *And God granted him that which he requested."*
> I Chronicles 4:10

My Brother, Tom

"But as many as received Him, to them gave he power to become sons of God, even to them that believe on His name:"

John 1:12

O n May 19, 2008 my wife dropped me off at Clara White Rescue Mission. I was scheduled to preach there. I had no concrete way of getting back home. I was not about to allow not having a ride home keep me from preaching. I was willing to catch a bus and hope the bus would get me close enough to Middleburg from Jacksonville. Somehow I believed that God would provide the ride I needed.

Shortly after I had finished preaching, a man walked into the Rescue Mission. He announced, "If you would like to go to church, the bus will leave for Middleburg in approximately fifteen minutes."

He also let those who would be riding the bus know that they would be given some food to eat. A sack lunch would be given to take with them after church. After this man finished his announcements, I went up to him and asked him, if I could get a ride to Middleburg on his bus. He said, "Yes."

During the bus ride to Middleburg, we prayed and sang gospel songs that were familiar to me. We were briefly introduced to the man who turned out to be my brother via the Lord. His name

is Brother Tom Giblin. He introduced some of his helpers, John
Bryan, George Alexander, and Brother Ed Frasier.

Brother Tom was the designated spoke person for God. I was
able to connect easily with Brother Tom. He tells it like it is. He
shared with those who rode the bus that before he dedicated his
life to Christ he had a particular problem. He shared that for the
past twenty years, God has given him the victory over this challenge.
Tom pointed out that it has not been easy just because he is a
Christian.

Tom shared with us about his son's delicate medical condition.
He also spoke about his concern for his daughter who has endured
some medical challenges. Tom spoke of his lovely wife who has
also endured some great physical adversities. Tom made it clear
that God has done some great things in his life.

One of the things that stood out to me that brother Tom shared
is this, 'we all have a story to tell'. All of us have problems, and we
need to tell people about what God has done for us. How God has
helped us through the problems of life.

I would like to offer a word of thanks to the minister of the
gospel who was instrumental in connecting me to my brother
Tom. This is Dr. Ken Pledger, the Pastor of Calvary Baptist Church
in Middleburg, Florida.

If I were standing next to my Brother Tom, many people would
have a hard time believing that Tom and I are truly bothers. To
be honest with you, I would be in the same predicament if I was
looking at this matter from a natural perspective. I am African
American and my brother Tom is not. If my brother Tom was
filling out a survey and was asked to write or circle the box that
best describes your race, he would have 'white' as his description.

Some of you may be wondering why is it that I took time out to
let you know that my skin color is dark and that brother Tom's is
light. The point is made because the color of Tom's skin nor mine
does not matter with God. He is my brother because he believes

that Jesus is God's Son. That Jesus died for our sin. That Jesus rose from the dead. By putting his trust or faith in God's word, he and all of those who put their trust in God are transformed into children of God.

> *"That if you confess with your mouth the Lord Jesus and believe in your heart that God has raised Him from the dead, you will be saved.*
> *For with the heart one believes unto righteousness, and with the mouth confession is made unto salvation."* Romans 10:9-10

In the book of Galatians there is a wonderful description that summarizes how God transforms human beings into children of God. Galatians 3:26-28 says,

> *"For ye are all the children of God by faith in Christ Jesus.*
> *For as many of you as have been baptized into Christ have put on Christ.*
> *There is neither Jew nor Greek, there is neither bond nor free, there is neither male nor female; for ye are all one in Christ Jesus."*

Needless to say this passage also speaks to skin color. God has no respect of persons. As believers, we are all one in Christ Jesus. It is in His power that we can transcend racial, gender, and cultural beliefs.

How Did She Do That?

Psalms 75:6-7

"For promotion cometh neither from the east, nor from the west, nor from the south. But God is the judge: he putteth down one, and setteth up another."

My daughter Jasmine shared with me on August 27, 2007 that she was going to be the valedictorian of her graduating class in 2008. Now being the loving father that I am, I believed Jasmine had the ability to be valedictorian. However, I did not know if she had the time to raise her grade average to be top of her class. You see, I did not want Jasmine to set herself up for a major disappointment. Furthermore, I did by no means want to convey to Jasmine that she could not have her dream.

The words that came to me for Jasmine are these. Do your best, and no matter what happens dad loves you. Do you know what happened? In May of 2008 a letter from my daughter's school arrived in the mail. The letter mentioned a lot of good things about Jasmine. The letter also informed my wife and me that our daughter Jasmine had indeed earned that noble position of being the valedictorian of her graduating class.

In June of 2008 Jasmine stood before her graduating class and delivered one of the most poignant speeches of the day.

Perhaps some of you who are reading this are saying Jasmine is your daughter, of course. You would see things that way. You could be right. However, I would like to think that my perception of Jasmine's delivery of her speech, with its inclusive, inspirational, courageous, and visionary components made her speech outstanding. To top things off, Jasmine had the audacity to thank God.

In December of 2009, Brother Matt and I had a discussion about education. I shared with Brother Matt that my two daughters attended one of the finest institutions of higher learning in the state of Florida. Brother Matt shared with me how he encouraged his oldest son to be the best at what he does. He pointed out that it is the duty of the parent to make sure their children obtain an education. Brother Matt helped me to realize that my daughters are blessed to have two parents that are college graduates.

Then Brother Matt asked a penetrating question. Do you think your daughters did well in school because of something special that was done in your home or do you think they could have been as successful in another environment? God is able to make you a success in spite of your life circumstances. It is because of the goodness of God that people are able to master life's challenge.

As a Christian parent, I see a dangerous tendency. We send our children to secular institutions where we hope their light of love and hope would shine the brightest, but it seems like a great deal of our children learn to master certain facets of art, science, and various other subjects and fail to maintain their faith in God as well.

To those Christian children who choose to attend a secular college, be true to God. Keep in mind there is nothing wrong in earning a degree from a secular school. However, don't start or continue to live a life style that contradicts your faith in God.

Ask yourself how did I do that? Make a choice to live out your faith. Remember, you are a Christian. Do your best to live like a Christian in a hostile environment. Keep in mind people are watching you. Make your Lord proud to call you His child.

Sister Eleanor's Prayer Of Faith

Sister Eleanor Hammond has been my partner at the rest home ministry service numerous times. She would go into the women's rooms and announce that we are from Harvest Dome Church. She would let the people know that the pastor of the church is Pastor R.J. Washington. Then she would ask the women if they would like prayer. Her next question was, "Can my brother in the faith come into your room and pray for you." Once permission was granted we would pray for those who made a request. When I went into the room where a male was residing, I would ask the same question of the men to permit my Sister Eleanor to enter. For the people who were not able to speak, a prayer was often made for their health and safety.

Now I was familiar with doing things this way, but then one day Sister Eleanor talked to me about ministering in an area that I had never been before. To complicate matters, the group she wanted to minister to was suffering from Alzheimer's. While I did not verbalize what was going on in my mind, I recall clearly thinking why on earth do you want to share the gospel with a group of people who may not understand what we are saying? I agreed to the suggestion made by Sister Eleanor. It turned out to be one of the most rewarding visits I have ever made to the rest home. I was able to see with my own eyes that when it comes to Alzheimer's, there are various stages or levels of loss. Regardless of whatever stage a person may be part of, people need to be loved and cared for throughout life. It is good to see people treated with love no matter what their plight in life.

> "... And Jesus answering said unto them, Have faith in God. For verily I say unto you, That whosoever shall say unto this mountain, Be thou removed, an be thou cast into the sea; and shall not doubt in his heart, but shall believe that those things which he saith shall come to pass; he shall have whatsoever he saith. Therefore I say unto you, What things soever ye desire, when ye pray, believe that ye receive them, and ye shall have them ..."

(Mark 11:22-24)

God blessed Sister Eleanor to guide me to the right people at the right time. This simple obedience resulted in God helping Sister Eleanor and me to lead a soul to Christ. We also were able to encourage a backslider to get her relationship with Christ in order.

AN ENRICHED LIFE

Colossians 3:17
*"And whatsoever ye do in word or deed, do all in the name of the Lord
Jesus, giving thanks to God and the Father by him."*

I am blessed with five children, three sons and two daughters.
They are Charles Jr., Charmaine, Jasmine, Jerome, and
Jamal. When I was released from the hospital in 2004, I was
unable to perform all of the activities of daily living without
the help from family, friends and others. My dear wife had the
daunting task of bathing me, and cleaning me up after using
the bathroom. I was dependent upon her to even help me get
dressed. Since I was unable to drive, she often took me to public
functions. My children have been and remain a great asset in the
area of help.

I recall falling down at home and not being able to get up off
the floor. My daughter Jasmine helped me to get off the floor. My
daughter Charmaine has helped me to get dressed and to comb
my hair and also put on my shoes. My sons Jerome and Jamal have
helped me to get dressed so often that the number of times is too
numerous to recall.

My oldest son, Charles Jr. was not aware of the severity of my
plight in regards to visually seeing and observing my condition. At
the time Charles Jr. was living in another state.

I am very appreciative for the help my family has rendered and continues to provide for me. Mere words are unable to convey the gratitude I have for them. I would like to offer a special note of thanks to my baby boy Jamal. In the midst of stress and strain, sacrifice and service Jamal exhibited a super generous spirit. He offered service with special care and as a consequence he was and is called on more often for help than his other siblings.

Kindness so far had been limited to family members, but family members were not the only ones to show me kindness. My family was not alone in helping to enrich my life. I would like to share some stories about people who are not related to me but have in a special way made my life richer.

David Langley made sure I had a ride home from my speech club meetings. He often went out of his way to make sure when he was not going to attend a meeting that someone would give me a ride home. David has not read this book yet, therefore, he is not aware of how powerful his acts of kindness are to me. However, one day the world will know how strong and powerful are simple acts of love.

Willie Clowers picked up the torch when David moved. Willie not only gave me rides to and from club meetings, he transported me to and from functions that were not held at our club. Willie also represents hope and inspiration to me. Willie had an accident that had left him temporarily paralyzed, but now he is able to drive a car and work full time. I consider Mr. Clowers to not only be my brother in the Lord, but he is viewed as a friend as well.

Minister Warren Hodge is a Christian of much love. I have seen with my own eyes his dedication and devotion to serving senior citizens and others. Minister Hodge has graciously assisted me in helping me with transportation and Christian growth. He too is a brother in the faith and a friend.

Brother Givens has shown me much encouragement. He like Mr. Clowers know the pain and agony associated with not having full control of one's body. Talking to brother Givens gave me another person I could relate to who not only had experienced pain, but moved on in life without allowing pain to keep him from serving and praising God.

Then, there is Mr. Khamil Ojoyo. He has been instrumental in providing me opportunities to serve humanity in a manner that lifted my spirit by allowing me to be part of a work that has eternal implications. There were times when the forces of darkness put stumbling blocks in my way, and I was unable to perform my duty as planned. I found myself in need of forgiveness, and God granted Mr. Ojoyo the power to forgive me. When you let down a person you respect it hurts. Thankfully, his understanding of my predicament made things right again. Out of all the work I have been blessed to be a part of, I rank the work of serving humanity associated with a particular rescue mission second to none.

Pastor Sylvester Small, his lovely wife, Dr. Lily Small and their children, Andy and Donna hold a special place in my life. It is he who ordained me and nurtured my growth by not only giving me ample opportunities to preach. He has given me his unconditional support and expressed to me his appreciation of the work God allowed me to do while under his care. Pastor Small, I am eternally grateful for your devotion to God, and for the love you have shown me and others.

Steve Brock and Jim Horton are two of my former classmates from West Coast Bible College who personified what it means to share their knowledge to help others. Mr. Roderick Bourgeois happens to be one of and perhaps the best friend I have in this world. Our friendship extends beyond two decades. We have been blessed to work together, and I am the godfather of his son, Dorian surely helps. We all need someone we can feel safe to share those rough areas of life without the fear of being ridiculed or put down. Roderick, I thank God that in you, God has given me a friend of the ages.

To my brothers in the faith Rev. Kenneth Blackwood and Rev. Tony Douglass, your encouragement and stimulating conversations and friendship has made me a more informed servant and a more appreciative one, as well.

Pastor Antonio Richardson, Reverend Oliver Simmons, Charlie Duvall, Debra Duvall, Sabrina, Joe Jr., Toyia, Mrs. Ophie and the late Joe Sr. have contributed to the sum total of who I am today.

In September of 2009 my wife took me to Titus Harvest Dome. I met a member there who had not seen me in a long time. This person said, "Hello"! She inquired if I had finished the book you are currently reading. At the time of course my reply was, "not yet." This precious lady is Sister Campbell. Her husband was the late David Campbell, who was a humble servant of God. Sister Campbell words were so encouraging to me. I thank God for her words of encouragement. Angelo offered unusual encouragement with these words, "I would like to read your book when you finish it."

Brother Noah Jackson made sure I got off the bus safely. He also saw that I crossed the busy street without being hit. He is another example of someone who cares.

Emma Givens from Detroit, Michigan assisted me in getting on the bus to return back to Jacksonville. She carried my lunch until I could find a seat. Another person, Keedrick from Alabama called my wife to let her know the bus was running late. The list could run on and on. God does enrich our lives through others in so many ways, be it in words or deeds. Thanks be to God for His numerous blessings. I have had an enriched life.

Brooks Love

Today I would like for you to join me on an amazing true love story. What makes this story so remarkable is the depth of love shown to its recipient. In order to grasp the deep level of love that is contained in this story, I would like for you to imagine walking into a hospital to receive an operation.

After the operation you awaken lying in your bed. Suddenly you realize that you lack complete control of your body. It dawns on you that you are in need of total care. Thanks to Brooks whatever I needed, Brooks was there to help me and care for my needs.

When I needed to get dressed in the morning for breakfast, Brooks made sure that someone was there to dress me. When breakfast was delivered, Brooks made sure that someone was there to feed me. Even when I screamed out in pain, Brooks made sure that someone took care of my pain.

Later when I was unable to walk, Brooks sent Shawn and others to help me develop the ability to stand up and eventually walk again. When I needed help in the bathroom, loving care was there to help me. Loving care even overlooked my messes to render me clean and refreshed.

During the course of my hospital stay my left hand was unable to perform its function. Again, Brooks sent someone to help. Brooks sent Sarah who helped me to learn to use my right hand to eat. I believe that I was blessed to have two care providers with the name of Sherry. One was a dedicated nurse and the other Sherry was a compassionate and extremely helpful person, my social worker.

Tony was the only male nurse that I recall caring for me during my stay at Brooks. He was good and concerned about me as a person. When I needed inspiration, I was provided a chaplain. The chaplain happened to be one of the most courageous persons I have ever met. This man of God had an appreciation for others that exemplify love.

The greatness of Brooks lies not merely in its ability to meet one's physical need. Brooks goes further and causes one to feel valued and appreciated as a person during their stay. I'd like to remind you that it is no easy task for a person to provide total care for another person day after day. This kind of loving care conveys to that person being helped, the message that you are loved and you are of great worth.

Now I hope my story regarding my life at Brooks will be an inspiration for those who took time to read it. However, if one day you find yourself in a hospital or a home and you are in need of total care; I hope you will be blessed to have the same type of love and care that I received while at Brooks Rehabilitation Center. Brooks exemplified love in deeds. I am reminded of the words about love in I Corinthians 13:4-8a:

> *"Charity suffereth long, and is kind; Charity envieth not; Charity vauntath not itself, is not puffed up. Doth not behave itself unseemingly, seeketh not her own, is not easily provoked, thinketh no evil; Rejoiceth not in iniquity, but rejoiceth in the truth; bareth all things, believeth all things, hopeth all things, endureth all things. Charity never faileth;"*
>
> (KJV)

My Final Thanks

My brother, Reverend James Fair is a minister of the gospel, and a pastor. I believe it was July of 2007 when he was scheduled to preach to a packed church of relatives and Christian brothers and sisters. However, when it came time to preach, he shared with me that he felt the Lord leading him to allow me to preach. Now I unlike a pastor of a church who preaches frequently, my opportunities to preach are not as numerous. I was extremely grateful to God for the opportunity to preach, and at the same time I was reminded of my human frailty. I felt inadequate for the task, but God was able to use what He had given me to tell those who were in attendance about the unconditional love of God. How Jesus was sent to redeem us from the grips of sin. By putting your trust in God, and accepting by faith that Jesus died and rose from the dead, and has made it possible for those who put their trust in Him to live forever. Live with peace and harmony with the creator of the universe. I am blessed to have a brother who is receptive and obedient to the leading of God.

Mrs. Caroline Simes is a gifted mother of two children, a dedicated wife, and one of the most energetic and caring persons I have ever met. I was able to detect the excitement in her voice as she shared with me how she was instrumental in helping to make the life of a certain lady better. This information she shared came from 'www.awarenotafraid.com', which is a business dedicated to

the safety of women, children, the disabled and other citizens of
need in our nation.

Mr. Willis is one of the expert trainers and master in this field
of study. This man is so talented that in less than a couple of hours
he can pass on some information and skills that can enable you to
be a more confident and safer person.

There are some natural things that people do to maintain and
sustain life. People eat, sleep, work, play and go to school.

People live in a society where other people in their community
seek to harm them. 'Aware Not Afraid' is an excellent place to
obtain life saving things that can enable you to enjoy some of those
natural things of life a while longer. This is because you can be
trained to prevent a misguided person from making you a victim.

I am compelled to mention Mrs. Willis. Her compassion moved
her to make sure that during training that I was provided comfort
of a chair when my body was in need of some relief, as a result
of my disability. The lack of physical safety can result in the loss
of life. My ultimate focus is on the eternal well being of those in
our society. However, I am mindful that without physical safety the
opportunity to share the gospel would be lost.

When I think of the generosity and love that has come my way
via Pastor Pledger, I am reminded of my natural siblings and family.
The deeds of love shown are too numerous to keep an accurate
count. I am thankful to God for allowing me to be served, to serve,
to be encouraged, to be trusted to trust, to love and to be loved.
Pastor Pledger has a remarkable gift to convey the gospel and to
in an amazing way conclude his sermons with God's love and the
consequences of refusing that love.

Calvary Baptist Church is blessed to have a precious gem in
Sister Pledger. Her beautiful smile and humble spirit are only a
few of the desirable traits that helped make her be so widely used
by God to be a help to others.

In addition, the following brothers in the faith: Tim, Chris, Art, Bolton, Walter, Doan, Larry, Spencer, Anthony, LeClare, are men of the church that have brought rays of sunshine into my life. The love of Brother George Alexander and his wife Dorothy is outstanding. Brother Henry Martin,

Roy Layton, Sr., and Roy Layton Jr. hold a special place in my life. Sister Mary Dusenbery, Brother Tom Betenbaugh,

Sister Shirley Betenbaugh all have been a tremendous help to the completion of this book.

There is a group of church members that I was blessed to work with on a regular basis. Brothers Ed Frasier, Tom Giblin, Daniel Williams, Bob Cunningham and Sister Pat Cunningham, and Sister Jennifer are dedicated servants for Jesus. Couples John and Melisa, Matthew and Jennilyn, and Brother and Sister Douglass and Brother and Sister Kite are symbols of decades of service for our Lord. Young people like Brother Ryan Pledger, Sister Cashel Brunette, Emmanuel Threatt, Thomas Arnold, Dominic, and Nate are zealous reminders to all of us that God is still using young people as His representatives.

Sister Addie Giblin and Brother Tom Giblin give new meaning to practical love in the midst of some of life's most difficult challenges. Your love for your family and for God inspires me. When faced with the hard times that will one day cease, and we pause and are mindful of the suffering of others. We will then realize that we are not alone in that part of life. As Christians we will one day live eternally with our Lord. In a real sense we are transitional people. Some of us are in a greater position of change than others, until we are moved from this world to our heavenly home. It is then that we no longer have to concern ourselves with things that change, but until then, let us serve God by helping those in need.

People like Mr. Douglas Hobbs, Mr. Andrew Sanford, Mr. Calvin L. Simmons, Mr. Terry Stewart and Brother Sean Nettles are people that I met in the state known for sunshine that helped to make my life brighter.

Noreen Belcher is known by many for her work in the area of vocational assistance and support. I have been honored to know her as a well educated professional, who is

dedicated to her work. Most importantly, she is able to convey that she cares about you as a person, which I believe is one of her most precious skills. Not everyone that earns a graduate degree and more education is able to transmit to others genuine concern. Noreen, as these words were typed a smile was on my face. Because of our training, some of us who are skilled in the realm of analysis are reluctant to open up and seek help in finding employment due to fear of being stigmatized and over analyzed. You are a credit to your profession, and I like for you to know that I deeply appreciate the work you do.

Michigan may be cold in the winter, but when it comes to love, Michigan has lakes of love that are second to none. In fact, people like Paul Johnson Sr., Paul Johnson Jr., Precious Johnson, Pierre Johnson, Eddie Fair, Jr., Dominique Fair, Mitchell Fair, Michael Fair, Eboni Fair, Barbara Fair, Latoya Fair, Parrish Fair, Mother Nellie Cole, Delores Fair, V. Fair, Jimmy Bullock, Tommie John, Phil Davis, Montez Boone, Ressie, Michael, Cindy, Joyce, Judy, Larry, Bugs, Freeman, Rafael, Billy, Damaian, and Janie can honestly say that they live in a State where there is a Lake Superior.

Mrs. Kim Baker is a Christian that loves people. Her love was expressed when she met a stranger in January of 2010. It happened in Jacksonville, Florida which is normally not known for having cold weather. However, when Kim reached out in love to help a stranger, it was very cold. The man in need had worn some loose fitting socks. It was so cold that the person in need of help did not realize his plight until he sat down and saw that his socks had literally slipped off his legs and down inside his shoes.

To complicate the matter in an attempt to correct the problem, I pulled off my shoes. In that process one of my socks came off my feet. I was not able to put that sock back on. Fortunately for me, a caring person was willing to stoop

   down and do for me what I was not able to do for myself. She put my sock on for me. She helped me straighten up my tie. Then she shared encouraging words regarding my concern about an appointment I was scheduled for.

I was impressed by the kindness she showed to a stranger. I learned that she was a sister in the faith, and that Jesus is Lord of her life. She remains a sister in the faith today. Once again, thank you Kim for helping me. By the way, you were right. God worked things out pertaining to my bus situation and my scheduled appointment.

There is a group of Christians from the Jacksonville area that are a tremendous blessing to me. Some of those individuals are John Brogan, Tyrone Reese, Tanya Jackson, Andre Fortune John, Robert Dell, Terrence Collins, and Rosalyn McKinnon. These are a small portion of the larger number of people from Jacksonville that attend Calvary Baptist Church. Another member of Calvary Baptist Church is Sister Rebie Holloway whose spirit of warmth and kindness is refreshing.

Other individuals who live throughout our nation are Sister Inez, Veronica, Myrtle Blackwood, Dawn and Brothers Sean Gay, Johnny Gonzales, and the twins Dwight and Dwayne all whose investment into my life is greatly appreciated.

Timothy McLain and Malik are two students from Everest University that took time out of their lives to listen to my story. I was able to tell them about the time in my life when I was totally dependent on others for survival, and how God has brought me a mighty long way. I believe both of you will be graduating in November of 2010. May God's mercy and grace abound in each of your lives!

Sister Bernadette Ellis, Mother Grace and the lovely Mother Harris and Charles W. Fair, Rachel, Celeste, Jayden C. Fair, and Williams all have been instrumental in enriching my life.

On April 22, 2010 I was blessed to attend an event in which my oldest daughter, Charmaine was presented her 'gold rope'. She had earned good grades during her final two

years through dedicated studying. Then on May 2, 2010 God allowed me to witness Charmaine's graduation ceremony. Military service or graduate school both are visions for your future. Keep God first in your life and you won't go wrong. Jerome, Jamal, Jasmine and Charles Jr. and Mona, I am proud of each of you.

Last, but not least, I want to say "Thank You !" to Brother and Sister Fryman, Patrice, Ricky Ladson, Nathaniel Pledger, Brother Weaver, Brother Reggie Dorsey, Sister Hockenhull, Sister McDonald, Elder S. Hart, Apostle Bobby Johnson, Sister April Washington, Brother Dan Babor, April Babor, Tevin Heath, Wheel Hicks, Roosevelt Hicks Jr., Barbara Ann, Vivian, Roland, Ricky, Mark, Sharon, Shari Smith, Brian Waytowtich, Joe, Sister Renee McNeil, Holly Moses, Brother Rick and Sister Gunthrop, John Chafffin, Sarah, Joshua, Melissa, Ryan, Caitlin, Brother Bruce, Sister Evette, Sister Olivia, Mr. James Walker Jr., Mr. Maurice Murray, Kayla Kierce, Maria Nash, Shanna Guthrie LMT, Brian McGouey, Mr. Nathaniel Turner, Mrs. Dana Turner, Lynn Fields, Hajra Bajric, Mr. Calvin Brown, Brandon M., Michelle Martin, Johnathan Lee, Lisa Lee, Mr. Ron Antolik, Jole, Brother Jared, Brittaney, Brother and Sister Simmer, Dantae, Stacy Enoch, Guil and Ruth Yates, Mr. Jamel Jefferson, Christian Harris, Brother Marv Robinson, Sister Robinson, Brother Jason Brunette, Sister Tiffney Brunette, Brother Greene, Sister Greene, Sister Faye, Brother Chaffin, Tina, Mr. Aaron Hicks B. Hicks Sheryl Walker Angelo Robinson, Mr. Jim McGahee, Sister McGahee, Hannah Jones, Mr. Dub Plyler, Jack Grove, Michael Baker, Brother Lambert, Sister Lambert, Sister M. B. Jackson,

Lucia Islas, Janelle Thomas, Mother Katie Grier, Mother Ruth Sykes, Harry Weldon, Mary L. Holt, Henry N. Vaughn Sr., Rodney Randle, Bernice Fair, Judge McCarter,

Gary Gunter, Vester Williams, Tommy Williams and Marvin Gardner. Jeff Robinson is a symbol of the best of the employees at Jacksonville Transportation Authority. You are all precious souls and instruments of God's mercy. There is an employee that works at the hospital in Orange Park that epitomizes what it means to care. You work in the area that performs CT scans. I don't know your name, but your kindness is amazing. Larry Bana and Sister Nancy De Marsh are blazing examples of how God can help people find what it really means to enjoy life, even if it means working with the precious homeless children of God.

On March 13, 2011 I heard a person give a testimony that touched the depth of my being. This person shared how their response to the death of a person that was dear resulted in their departure from following the path of righteousness, which is rooted in Jesus. However, while this person was off the straight and narrow path the people of God never gave up on this person, and now this person has grown closer to God. This person is sorry for the pain caused to relatives and friends, and yearns that their love ones will experience the love of God, that is found in John 3:16. People often journey to various locations and no trip or experience is as significant as accepting God's love because God promised to forgive those who accept Jesus as their Lord. Jesus died and rose again I urge you to receive God's love.

On March 17, 2011 I was blessed to meet Sister Lois Appleton. She helped me cross safely one of Jacksonville's dangerous streets. Lois has a great appreciation for God's mercy. We have this Godly connection. God has been good to us. He has brought us through some very difficult days. Sister Pearlie Medina, you are loved.

On March 25, 2011 Mrs. Delores Beamon inspired an audience. She delivered a speech which dealt with the beauty that comes from life's struggles. When people deal appropriately with life difficulties they produce some of the most beautiful and gifted people you may ever meet. Thank you, Delores for sharing your life with others. Hearing you helped me realize how blessed I am, even though I've faced a lot of struggles.

Sister Rita Allen, Pastor Gaudette, Sister Gaudette, Brother and Sister Soprano, Ivey Summey, Brother James Smith, Mr. Sylvester Smith, Jacklyn Smith, Timmy Harris, Beverly, Lionel, Leroy, Earl, Elroy, Laurie, Kareem, Dejanique, Demeiko, Shalaina, Berril, Sherril, Billy Marell, Sister Alice Waugh, Jay C. Thomas, Chislon Thomas, Ariel Thomas, you are loved.

On March 26, 2011 Sister Maude B. Jackson graciously allowed me to participate in the building of a dream. This kind act opened the door for me to meet soap maker, Brother Bill Jackson, Claude W. Bass III, Sister Lena Lewis and many family and friends of the late Mr. Cyrus Forrester.

Sister Denny Randolph represents a large number of women who endure the pain of being separated from a spouse who is serving in the military. It was an honor to meet you and your cousin Harry at church.

Larry Fair, thanks for the love you showed me and my family. Mr. Roosevelt Hicks Sr. thanks for not giving up on me when I was in poor health.

Cousin Debra from Starkville, Mississippi thank you and your husband for being so kind to my dad before he passed away. Brother Kent, Sister Kent, Brother Eddie Smith Jr., Brother Robert S. Lee, Brother Todd Marsh, Sister Jennifer Bodary, Brother Wheeler, Sister Wheeler, Brother Ramsey, and Sister Ramsey you have all enriched my life.

Faye Hicks, Russell Richardson Berenice Hicks, Viviene Fair, Matt McMullin, Brother Hood, Sister Hood, Brother Chuck, Brother Chris Wills, Don Haynes, Sister Carly, Sister Angie, Dr. Samuel Louis-Jean, thanks for your support.

Brother Walter St. Clair (WWII Veteran), thank you for being a precious friend. On 1/22/11, I received a phone call from my brother Eddie. He told me that my father had died. That took me by surprise. I knew that my dad was very sick but I did not think he would die as soon as he did. I had just spoken with him during the early part of January 2011. He sounded so strong and alert. If there was ever a time that a person needed to experience Missouri, that time was now. In the midst of this great loss, the Fair siblings and other family members and friends reached out in love in an amazing way to bring about healing and comfort that was needed. I thank God for love. Thank you so kindly brother Burns, Sister Barbara Fair, and Sister Delores Fair for taking my dad to Missouri before he died. The memories of the love you showed my dad means so much to me. Jaclyn Sluka is a devoted mother. She would like to leave these words "Never give up, things could always be worse. Everything will always get better." Timmy Morris would like for us to know that 'I'm a child of God with a master plan.' Mr. Reynold D. Peterson is more than a great engineer; he is concerned about the least of those in society. He reached out and helped me, thank you Mr. Peterson.

About The Author

The author, Charles E. Fair was born in the late 1950's in the segregated South. During his boyhood he moved with his family to the North. It was there that Charles had a life changing encounter with a nice white neighbor. Unknowingly her acts of kindness shattered his stereotype beliefs that all white people are bad.

Charles Fair continued his education by attending West Coast Christian College and the California State University at Fresno where he completed his Masters Degree in Social Work. During this time Charles met and married a young lady, Ramona who was his classmate. They have been married for over twenty-six years. They have five children of which some are in college and some are in their teens.

During his arm service time Charles served as a medical specialist in the army. Charles has served his community in California and Florida as a Social Worker for many years. He also worked in Child Protection Services. Charles was also ordained as a minister in 2001.

Relaxation has come for Charles in the form of reading and at many times a quiet spot to fish. He always has time for his family. As a child he was extremely shy. That is hard to believe when viewing him as a public speaker. One of his past times is with the Toast Masters Club. One would think that his favorite speeches are those of the late Dr. Martin Luther King, Jr.

Life is not without some set backs of some nature. Charles has had his own when after surgery in 2004 he awaken to the fact that he was seriously paralyzed and could not move all of his body parts. A new life began. A struggle little by little of progress to regain his ability to move his limbs and finally walk again with assistance of a cane. He has a story to tell. You will read part of it in the pages of this book.

www.ingramcontent.com/pod-product-compliance
Lightning Source LLC
Chambersburg PA
CBHW061227280526
45784CB00006B/2667